ADVFN Guide:
A Beginner's Guide
to
Value Investing

CLEM CHAMBERS

CONTENTS

Investing: How to Get Started   1

Why Value Investing?   3

Searching for Companies   6

Criteria   10
Financial Criteria 1: P/E   11
Financial Criteria 2: Divident Yield   14
Financial Criteria 3: 50% Fall From Share Price High   17
Financial Criteria 4: Directors Purchasing   19
Financial Criteria 5: Cash in the Bank   23
Financial Criteria 6: Sales to Market Cap   26
Financial Criteria 7: Equity   29

No-Nos!   32
No-No 1: Family Firms   33
No-No 2: Government Footballs   34
No-No 3: Financial Restatements   35
No-No 4: Legal Outcome   36

Value investing: How To Do It In Practice   37
Step 1: Build a Portfolio   37
Step 2: Portfolio Size   40
Step 3: Making a Selection   41
Step 4: Buying Shares   48

A Few Other Issues   50
Issue 1: Investing Costs   50
Issue 2: Charts   51
Issue 3: Selling   52
Issue 4: Compounding   53

Conclusion   55

About the Author   57

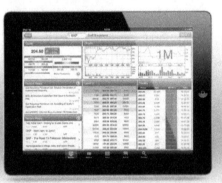

Investing: How To Get Started

Most people think that investing in stocks and shares is a risky game only played by rich people and gamblers.

From the outside it seems it's hard to know how to make money investing in stocks. There are so many stories about people who lose their shirts.

This is true and false depending on what you set out to do.

Investing is not hard but trading shares is nigh on impossible.

Most people confuse the two things: trading is not investing and vice versa.

Trading is very close to gambling and, like betting on horses, it is extremely difficult to make a profit from that kind of activity.

Investing, on the other hand, is quite boring and the more boring you can make it, the better.

Investing is not hard. Making money by investing is not that difficult, but it takes effort.

There are many trading schemes, none of which I'm aware are much good at making money.

There are quite a few investing strategies and most will make you money. The simplest and the most tried and tested is value investing.

Value investing as a method was laid out clearly for the first time by an American professor called Benjamin Graham in the 1950s and one of his students, Warren Buffett, used it as the basis for his career in which he has become the richest man in the world.

Value investing is at its heart simple: buy cheap stocks then sell them when they are not cheap any more.

While value investing won't make you the richest person on the planet, it is a platform for good investment profits. The basics can be potted down into a set of simple straightforward methods.

I have followed the principles of value investing for many years and it has always given me excellent profits.

Apart from excellent profits, one key benefit of value investing is that it doesn't stress the investor out. Done properly it is a comfortable way to take risks with your cash.

Most stock market trading and investing ideas are packed with stress and even when these systems are doing well, anyone following such ideas can be put through the emotional wringer. This emotional price is simply not worth paying for most people; it burns them out and dulls their desire to be involved.

The low stress level of a sensible investing strategy is a sign that the investment style you are following is a solid one. Investing should not feel like war, it should just be a normal working endeavour that takes a certain amount of time and effort. It shouldn't be a battle that keeps you awake at night.

Value investing is and should be quite an easy-going way to make money from the stock market.

Being dull doesn't make value investing popular like trading, but it does mean that those that follow this idea make money year in and year out while traders come and go.

Why Value Investing?

If you wish to double your money very quickly in stocks and shares, you should stop reading this book right now. This book is about getting rich slowly, not quickly.

Over twenty years value investing will build wealth, but you will not be rich from it in a couple of years.

A lot of people that trade the markets want to get huge profits, 100% or more in a year. This is basically impossible even if it might seem on the face of it achievable.

You have as much chance of doubling your money every year for three years as hitting a jackpot at Vegas.

To the nearest percentage there is no chance of earning gains like 100% a year from shares and if someone does, they have been very lucky and are not responsible for their good luck. Anyone reading this who has achieved such gains should close their positions now, pile their money up on a table and count it out before putting it back into the market. It will be a good opportunity to kiss their money goodbye. Luck or 'one way' markets that provide such profits do not last.

Value investing is a technique that when combined with the simple basics of investment provides a basis for building up wealth, with a lot less anxiety than the other investment strategies out there.

Its sixty year history is alone a strong recommendation that value investing works and will keep on working.

Other ideas have come and gone, yet value investing keeps on going.

One of the reasons for this longevity is that value investing requires discipline and some work. It is rather boring and unflashy.

This is a benefit but for many it is a drawback. People are drawn to risky games—and the stock market is considered risky—and they like excitement and kudos. These 'punters' want to make quick money because they have a gambling streak.

Value investing does not satisfy the gambling urge very much as it is quite drab, rather unexciting and takes regular maintenance. Gamblers want minimal work and plenty of sensation.

Value investing is like gardening, just the sort of thing that gamblers aren't interested in.

Consequentially value investing is never in fashion. However, because it makes money, it is never out of fashion either.

Most investors know they should be value orientated but few can resist the enticing whirligig of trading and the glamour of go-go shares.

This is understandable.

People simply can't resist the lure of the casino either.

Why else would people pour their money away on simple games like roulette, when they have worked so very hard earning the money in the first place? It is because people love noise, thrills and flashing lights. They get hypnotised by them. Many shares in the stock market are like casino games and the city has learnt long ago that most of their potential customers don't want sensible profits; they want the lure of riches and a gambling high.

Sadly greedy gambling kills in the stock market—or at least costs the player a bundle.

Meanwhile, diligence pays.

This is why value investing works. The market has to pay investors a good return to own boring out-of-fashion shares. Prices of unloved companies fall until they are so cheap that smart investors can't resist buying them. At some point this unpopularity goes into reverse and those that bought in cheaply make good returns.

If I turn that idea around you will quickly see why so many investors lose money.

The reverse situation is that people buy fashionable stocks that everyone loves. Clearly at some point the price of the share rises so high that people can't resist taking their profits. At this point everyone who can buy has already bought and therefore the share price must fall. When the company's share price falls it suddenly becomes less popular as holders start to lose money. Losses are made by everyone. As the price falls so the company gets more unpopular until no one wants to own it. After several rounds of this the share becomes ignored and cheap.

Enter the value investor.

The fundamental principle of value investing is the simplest: buy low, sell high. I like to say buy cheap and sell 'not cheap.'

The rest of this book is about how to do just that. Value investing is not a great deal of fun, it is not very exciting, but it will make you money. You can spend the profits later on fun exciting things.

(NB. Actually I think value investing is great fun, but I am probably weird. Hunting out value is an amusing challenge. You feel like a bit of a Sherlock Holmes weighing all the evidence and once you are confident in your skills it's amusing to note people unable to grasp simple facts that make the profit potential of a stock significant. However, I know as the CEO of ADVFN, one of the biggest share information websites in the world, that I am in a very small minority. It is like being a bird watcher rather than a football spectator. Market theory suggests this is yet another reason why value investment is so profitable. Few apply its rules.)

Searching for Companies

The key to value investing is finding companies that are cheap. That means looking for them. This might seem obvious but most people do not look for stocks, they listen to tips.

It is a mistake to take tips. Taking tips is the same as throwing your money down the drain.

Simply, never take notice of tips. At worst, use tips as a starting place for your research. If you will do that you will find that tips do not fit your criteria ninety-nine times out of a hundred.

It gets worse: if a tip makes you money—and few will—you won't have earned it and will have learnt nothing; it will be the financial equivalent of a snack on junk food. If you lose your money—and you very likely will—you will most likely lose a friend.

Just say no to tips and start looking for shares yourself.

Stock picking is all about developing the skill of searching for, identifying and monitoring stocks.

A few years back this would be a long, tedious and frustrating job. Good information on shares was really hard to find and when you found such data, it was expensive and after you bought it, it was very laborious to sieve through.

Thanks heaven for the internet and more particularly ADVFN.

I run ADVFN and I use it for all my investing. As such I'm not going to list all the many other places to go and find share information. ADVFN does the job for me.

Sites like ADVFN give you share information resources that in the 1990s would have cost you many thousands of pounds a year and in some cases tools that were simply not available.

This screenshot is for ADVFN's FilterX, which is an ultra-powerful tool to select, grade, sieve and separate shares on the stock market out of a universe of more than 2,000 in London alone.

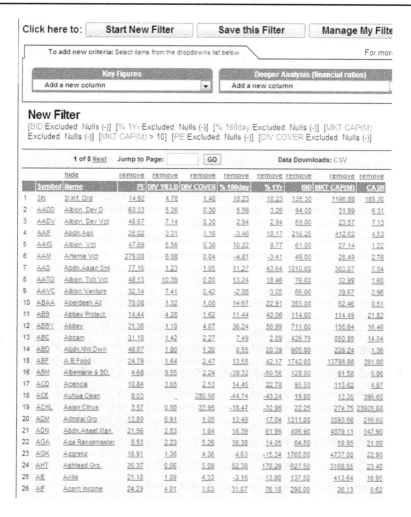

	Symbol	Name	PE	DIV YIELD	DIV COVER	% 180day	% 1Yr	BID	MKT CAP(M)	CASH
1	3N	3I Inf. Ord	14.92	4.78	1.40	10.23	10.23	135.30	1196.88	185.30
2	AADD	Albion. Dev D	63.33	5.26	0.30	5.56	3.26	94.00	31.99	6.31
3	AADV	Albion. Dev Vct	46.67	7.14	0.30	2.94	2.94	69.00	23.57	7.13
4	AAIF	Abdn Asn	26.92	3.31	1.16	-3.46	18.17	216.25	412.62	4.53
5	AAIG	Albion. Vct	47.69	5.56	0.38	10.22	8.77	61.00	27.14	1.22
6	AAM	Artemis Vct	275.00	8.08	0.04	-4.81	-3.41	49.00	28.49	2.76
7	AAS	Abdn.Asian Sml	77.16	1.23	1.05	11.27	43.64	1010.00	383.97	7.04
8	AATG	Albion. Tch Vct	48.13	10.39	0.20	13.24	18.46	76.00	32.99	1.60
9	AAVC	Albion Venture	32.14	7.41	0.42	-2.88	3.05	66.00	39.67	2.96
10	ABAA	Aberdeen All	70.08	1.32	1.08	14.67	22.91	355.00	52.46	0.51
11	ABB	Abbey Protect.	14.44	4.28	1.82	11.44	40.06	114.00	114.49	21.82
12	ABBY	Abbey	21.36	1.10	4.07	36.24	50.99	711.00	156.64	16.46
13	ABC	Abcam	31.10	1.42	2.27	7.49	2.09	426.75	850.85	14.04
14	ABD	Abdn.NW.Dwn	46.07	1.80	1.20	0.55	20.39	905.00	228.24	1.36
15	ABF	A.B.Food	24.79	1.64	2.47	13.55	42.17	1742.00	13798.88	391.00
16	ABM	Albemarle & BD.	4.68	9.55	2.24	-39.32	-50.56	128.00	61.58	5.06
17	ACD	Acencia	10.84	3.65	2.53	14.45	22.78	95.50	113.62	4.97
18	ACE	Auhua Clean	0.03		230.50	-44.74	-43.24	19.00	13.35	395.60
19	ACHL	Asian Citrus	3.57	0.80	33.95	-18.47	-32.96	22.25	274.75	23925.88
20	ADM	Admiral Grp	13.80	6.91	1.05	13.49	17.04	1311.00	3593.66	216.60
21	ADN	Abdn.Asset Man.	21.56	2.83	1.64	16.39	61.96	406.90	4879.11	347.90
22	AGA	Aga Rangemaster	8.53	2.23	5.26	16.38	14.05	84.50	59.05	21.00
23	AGK	Aggreko	16.91	1.36	4.36	4.63	-15.34	1760.00	4737.00	22.90
24	AHT	Ashtead Grp.	35.37	0.56	5.09	52.38	170.29	627.50	3168.55	23.40
25	AIE	Anite	21.18	1.09	4.33	-3.16	13.80	137.50	413.64	16.95
26	AIF	Acorn Income	24.29	4.01	1.03	31.07	76.18	298.00	26.13	0.62

There is one for US and Canadian shares too. If you know what kind of company you are looking for, FilterX can drag those shares out of the pack in a matter of minutes rather than through hours of manual paperwork work.

It a real boon.

The internet is the best thing to happen for the private investor, period, and the funny thing is, most share traders couldn't care less about the facts and figures on the shares they follow, they want tips. They want to get rich quick.

Sadly instead they get poor fast.

On the other hand, professional investors use tools like FilterX, so the select group of conscientious private investors are in a small segment of the overall market when they use their own research to select stocks, and this puts them at an advantage over speculators who chase tomorrow's big riser or people that follow the research or tips of others.

Another key advantage to value investing is that many companies you will find that meet the right criteria are too small for institutional investors to chase, so you and a few other investors may be the only ones following these stocks. By finding such a stock you are getting in at the ground floor of an upwards move, an advantage that adds to your upside.

Of course, to select a stock you have to have some criteria. Beginners don't have any and in fact might not understand what all the mumbo-jumbo in a company's financial information means.

Don't worry, you would be truly horrified if you knew how few have any clue what many of a company's business metrics actually mean. This is hard to believe, but pretty soon you will note that when you read articles about shares, little is mentioned about the financial figures of the business and when they are, little detail is considered.

This is because it is boring. Boring doesn't sell newspapers or for that matter shares. What sells is hope. Words sell, not numbers. As they say in the US, don't sell the steak, sell the sizzle.

As someone interested in quality steak you can buy it cheap when it's raw.

Few people care about the financial facts, even if that is exactly what they should be watching. This is a part of human nature that gives smart diligent investors an edge.

As a proper value investor you will have your criteria which you will tune over time. You will come up with a few extra rules as you go along and hopefully that will improve your profits further.

It is your criteria and the tools you use that will determine your stock picking; tips will have nothing to say in the matter.

A value investor has a plan and sticks to it.

That plan should be that a share meets a set of criteria and that the criteria must be drawn from the basis of an investment idea. A value investor doesn't have to buy every value investment company that comes along, they should collect the strongest. They should buy the best of the best, a share that stands out.

When deciding to take the plunge to buy a share, remember the gold miners' saying, "If you think it's gold it isn't. If you know it's gold it is."

It also must be remembered that when you start on this journey you may end up with a large group of companies to pick through. Don't worry, there is no rush to buy, tomorrow is as good a day to buy as today or next week.

The stock market will always be full of prospects. What is more, as months pass you will learn about different companies and you will start to know which are good choices and which are risky or hopeless. Over time your skill and knowledge will build, so it is OK to start slow and build slow. Investing is a means to an end not an end in itself. Take your time.

Criteria

The following seven criteria are the keys to how you should start sieving down the thousands of stocks you have to choose from to find the shares you want to own.

Every day some shares will rocket up and some will slump down. As such some shares will disappear off the list and some will appear. Some will get more attractive and some less so.

With tools like FilterX, you can throw away all the stocks in the market that don't pass all these tests and you can then evaluate the shares that have run this gauntlet and only pick the juiciest candidates.

You will rarely run out of choice.

If you miss one this week, more will come along next week. The choice will thin in a bull market and you will be spoilt for choice in a crash. In the end, the criteria must be your pole star to navigate the stock market. Leaving the course set by the criteria is full of peril and may well doom your enterprise completely.

Do not worry that you are throwing away amazing companies that will boom when you filter the market. Unless you have a way of sieving for super companies, the duds you dredge up as well will more than counteract the occasional profitable rockets.

You want a high success rate and you want to have a good reason why the method you are using works. This is why value investing is such a good way to make money. Meanwhile getting lucky very rarely leads to getting wealthy in the stock market.

Financial Criteria 1: P/E

P/E stands for Price Earnings. Roughly speaking it means: how many years profit does it take to buy the company.

Expensive stocks have high P/Es. It is not uncommon for P/Es to hit 30, 50 or much more if the company is the flavour of the month.

A P/E of 14 is about normal. That means a normal profitable company makes profits equivalent to 1/14 of the price you would pay for the whole shebang if you could buy up all its shares at the current price and own the whole business.

The current value of a company is what many financial ratios revolve around. This key value is called Market Capitalisation, Market Cap or MKT Cap for short.

If you take today's share price and multiply it by the total shares it has issued to shareholders, you get the company's Market Cap.

Let's take an example from January 2012:

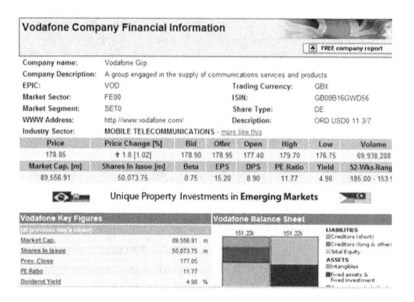

Vodafone has 50 billion shares.

Vodafone has a share price of 178.85 pence.

Market Cap is therefore 50 billion x 178.85 pence, which is 89.5 billion pounds.

That's a lot of money.

Now it has a P/E of 11.77.

This is because the share price is 178.85 and the profits of the company (EPS) are 15.2p a share.

P/E is therefore 178.85 divided by 15.2 which gives the P/E value of 11.77.

So if you bought the company, the company would take 11.77 years, at the current rate, to earn back what you paid for it.

Clearly this is better than waiting twenty-five years.

As such, the lower the P/E is, the more attractive or cheap the company can be.

If you were buying a sweet shop you wouldn't have to pay much more than a 3 P/E, because small businesses are thought of as precarious. If you were selling an internet business which was exploding with growth, 100 P/E might be in order. However, if the market average is 14, then anything below may be cheap.

There are pitfalls of course. The future is not certain and a company may not be able to carry on turning in good profits. A company that last year did well and earned a low P/E may have imploded this year leaving its P/E just a legacy from better times. In that case the next figure will show a different picture all together.

It can get even trickier when people use predicted future earnings to come up with a P/E, as often happens in the US, with a so called leading P/E.

All good criteria have their drawbacks, which is why we use a number of criteria together and why we check and double check to make sure we don't make any mistakes with our stock picking. By carefully covering as many angles as possible we increase our chances of being right and making money.

For example, you can pull up the company's previous performance and you can read all its news, so you can unpack the company's story and decide for yourself if the P/E is low for a good reason or low because the company is cheap. This is where you develop your skill and increase the profit you can make.

So what value of P/E should you look at?

Anything below 10.

Anything below a 10 P/E is interesting. Below 10 is value investing territory. You might look at shares below 12 if there was a big bull market making everything expensive, but generally you shouldn't bother.

A P/E of 10 is a good ceiling. The lower the better—7 or 8 P/E tends to be ideal, but in a crash P/Es can get a lot lower, so anything above 1 should get a check.

In normal markets anything below a 3 will turn out to be a dead company that has just imploded. However, they are still worth a look over. The nearly dead companies are just the sort of shares you want to learn how to spot. Do a post mortem; learn what a stock exchange disaster looks like and how it got there.

Some companies can be written off for dead but if you look very closely, they have a chance of surviving. This kind of company can be a big winner but they are very dangerous.

You should check them out but they will most likely fail the selection process. The other criteria you will be searching with will probably weed them out, but sometimes they won't.

A P/E of around 7 or 8 is a sweet spot; things generally get dicier under 5.

Remember the lure of excitement and greed is not your friend, yet once again you should look and study closely if criteria are met.

Recap Criteria 1

A value investor should throw away all companies whose P/E is above 10 and below 1.

Financial Criteria 2: Dividend Yield

If a company pays dividends, you get a payment from the company simply for being a shareholder. You do nothing and the money comes your way. This money cannot be taken back.

Prices rise and fall, but dividends only fall on your doormat. They are a strong sign that the company has profit and money and in the main, the value of the money paid out to you twice a year does not drag the company's share price lower in the long term.

If a company's share price is 100p and it pays out 10p in dividend then its Dividend Yield is 10%.

In this example you get a 10% pay-out of the company's value every year. It comes from the profits the company is making. That is, after all, what companies were invented for.

This dividend is normally paid out twice a year; a smaller interim dividend and a fat final dividend pay-out. There is such a thing as a special dividend too when a company pays out a one-off dividend. This is not common but it happens.

Here is an example: the insurance giant Aviva.

This company is paying out a cool 7.13% dividend and, besides, has a 7 P/E.

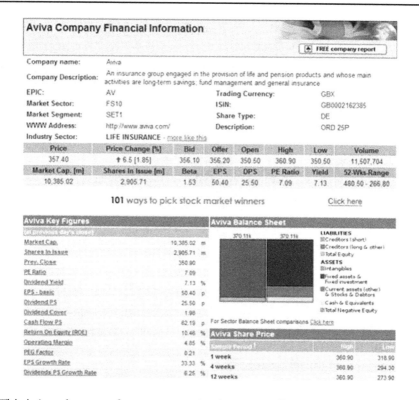

This is just the sort of company a value investor will be reading up on.

So what parameters are we sieving the stock market for when we look at Dividend Yield?

Cut out companies with a dividend yield less than 3%.

This is a pretty high hurdle to climb. In an era of low interest rates, 3% is a nice return. Less than that is a bit mundane. You could drop the figure low if you are short of stocks to pick but 3% is a good cut off point to start with. You are of course cutting out all those companies not paying a dividend at all. Remember you are playing Scrooge here. Who needs small dividends, bah humbug!

Cut out companies with a dividend yield above 10%.

If a company has more than a 10% dividend, the chances are the company has imploded. Just like a low P/E, a company with an enormous dividend based on last year's pay-out may be in terrible trouble. Exceptions to this are very rare. Such dividend yields appear to be huge because a company has hit the rocks and its share price has utterly collapsed, say, from 100p to 7p. Therefore last year's 1% dividend now looks like a 15%

dividend.

The bad news is the company is sunk and is not going to pay another dividend, so the high dividend is a mirage.

Once again you need to read the news about the company on ADVFN, go back a few years of history and try to work out the story of the firm. Check the share price chart to see if it tanked in a day or fell away over years and maybe check up on the bulletin boards in case the gossip gives you an insight into the 'behind the scenes' story. Make sure the reason a dividend is high is not because the company is crumbling into bankruptcy. Judge whether the company is going to pay out this year and is likely to pay out next year too.

Recap Criteria 2

A value investor should pick companies with a dividend yield between 3% and 10%.

Financial Criteria 3: 50%
Fall From Share Price High

The classic criteria for selecting value stocks is that the share has more than halved in recent history—that could be in the previous year or even three to five years.

The idea is that if the company's business hasn't changed much, or perhaps it might even have improved, then the share price fall is not based on the company's business but on some other factor.

There are many reasons a share price can fall. There can be a big seller trying to turn his shares into cash. This can be a founder's estate or a fund that is a forced sell due to technical factors. A whole sector can be out of favour and as the investment industry flips into the next hot sector, the stocks they are selling get smashed. The reasons for a falling share price can be many and varied. The trick is to find stocks hammered down for no good reason at all.

This is one of the factors people don't like about value investing: they have to buy dorky stocks. People will often say to me, "Why buy that share? It is going bust."

When you ask why, they say, "It is obvious because the share price has fallen so far."

It might be true, but the share price won't tell you; however, things like the P/E, dividend yield, and its sales performance etc. will.

Yet not many people start from this more numerate standpoint; instead they go with the flow and buy rising stocks everyone says are amazing and avoid anything unpopular.

Again they will invest in tips and opinion rather than the financial numbers. This makes life much easier for the value investor who is in effect operating scientifically or at least more scientifically than those driven by rumour, tips and hearsay.

You can of course only select companies that have fallen 60% or more, or 40%, but 50% is a good benchmark and it will cut out a lot of shares from your selection universe. You can take one year or three or five. With a tool like ADVFN's FilterX you can play around with all the parameters and focus in on the sweet spot of the market that looks most fruitful.

Recap Criteria 3

A value investor should pick companies that have fallen 50% from a medium term high.

Financial Criteria 4: Directors Purchasing

People are often impressed by public company directors. A PLC director is a high status and highly paid position. Yet company directors put their underpants and panties on one leg at a time like the rest of us.

Having met hundreds I can tell you they are just like everyone else in their ways.

Just like most people they don't want to waste their money. Just like most of us, they aren't rolling in money. They might earn a lot but like most things to do with money, the more you have the more you need and buckets of spare cash is a rarity even amongst the so-called rich.

So when directors puts their hands in their own pocket and buy stock in the company they runs, it is because they are dead certain they will make money out of that investment.

The interesting thing is that when directors buy shares in their own companies they have to tell the stock exchange so people can see them do it. This is to stop them getting up to monkey business, not of course that that could ever happen. This is what people mean by transparency. You can see what they are up to. Directors buy and of course they sell too.

These 'directors' buys' are a very useful tool as the announcement in effect tips the hand of what the directors think about the future prospects of their company.

No one knows better what the prospects of a company are than the people running it. They know the good news first and they know the horrible truth about how messy their business really is under the bonnet. They know what's going on from the crow's nest to the bilges. They have such a good grasp of the potential of the businesses they run that they are banned from buying or selling for a large part of the year and have to go through a fair amount of paperwork just to do a trade.

Directors don't like to lose money holding shares in their own company either, so 'directors buying' and 'directors selling' are important selection criteria in the decision of outsiders like us to buy and sell shares.

These days there are many ways directors can get shares in the company they run, so actually writing a fat check for shares is a big vote of confidence in the business. The more they buy of their own stock, the bigger the thumbs up. Also there is more than one director in a public company and these days wives and important people in the firm have to tell the stock exchange what they've done too. This means if a few directors are loading up on shares it's a strong signal the future of the company is bright. The more of them are buying, the better.

Of course like all signals there are exceptions. Directors know that people are watching their buying so if they think things look dicey they may buy some shares to help prop up the share price, but they won't buy many. A small sub-£5,000 buy may be token, especially if the director is earning a fat pay packet.

Sometimes when a company is right out of cash and luck, the directors will buy shares to put some money into the company. If the company is out of cash it is worth wondering whether this is the case.

Sometimes the director can be mad and have a history of buying shares all the way down as the company folds. You need to check the RNS (Stock exchange regulatory news).

This is an example of what a screen of Vodafone news looks like:

Here is an example of RNS about Vodafone, in this example some financial results:

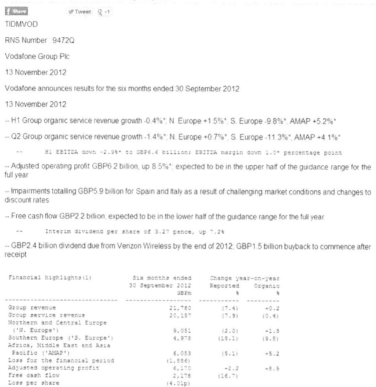

In amongst the news you will find an RNS called 'Directors'/PDMR shareholdings' (PDMR is an acronym for 'Person discharging managerial responsibility').

What you want to read about is purchases or sales of shares by the directors and you can ignore grants and gifts of shares by the company to its people as not relevant to this criterion.

When you find out about the buying and selling of shares by officers of a company you have a good idea of its prospects.

As such the value investor needs to check the details and balance the likelihood that the buys are simple straightforward purchases in a company because the director knows the business is worth a lot more than the current share price suggests.

Recap Criteria 4

Are directors buying, how many of them have and how much are they spending? The more the better.

Financial Criteria 5: Cash in the Bank

A share with a low P/E and a high dividend can be and often is also one that is on the ropes. That's fine in itself but the company must have the fuel to fight back to have a chance to win.

A dying company that has just imploded can fit a lot of the criteria that select a value investment but also be on its way into bankruptcy. We want to avoid that stock. However a company with a pile of cash can live to fight another day and make a comeback and a fat return.

When a business is out of cash, it is out of luck.

A business can even be in great shape, but if it has no cash to pay wages it's game over. That's common sense. Value investing is all about common sense. Value investing is about having several common sense rules and combining them to focus in on potential winners.

A company that is said to be in trouble can be just fine if it has a pile of cash to buffer it from its problems. This is exactly the kind of company we want to look into.

While some companies can be strapped for cash, others have more cash in the bank than the company is worth. This might seem ridiculous but it happens time and again. In fact it is not uncommon at all.

When a company is out of fashion and down on its luck, a good cash pile is a safety net and the bigger the pile the stronger the protection it has from a terminal accident.

For simple selection criteria any company with less than a million pounds of cash should be cut out of the group to research. This is being kind so as to leave in certain small companies that might be a good selection. However, you could make the cut at £10 million or even £50 million in cash. Wherever you put the cut, this will dispense with a lot of companies.

The more cash you demand the more likely the business is sound. There is no rocket science in that assumption.

Later on you can revisit the selections and trace the cash balances over the last few years. Any company haemorrhaging giant amounts of cash will stand out and you can dump them or mark them down when you come to the final selection.

Here is a random screen shot showing how you can track cash using ADVFN's Financials page:

Watch out for new tools and services! **View our new Historical Fundamentals** CLICK HERE

Amec Fundamentals

	31 Dec 2009 (GBP)		31 Dec 2010 (GBP)		31 Dec 2011 (GBP)		31 Dec 2012 (GBP)	
turnover	2,539.10	100.00%	2,950.60	100.00%	3,261.00	100.00%	4,158.00	100.00% m
pre tax profit	203.50	8.01%	258.20	8.75%	259.00	7.94%	263.00	6.33% m
attributable profit	171.70	6.76%	231.00	7.83%	232.00	7.11%	216.00	5.19% m
retained profit	121.40	4.78%	172.90	5.86%	146.00	4.48%	118.00	2.84% m
eps - basic	52.50		70.90		70.80		68.50	
eps - diluted	51.50		69.30		69.30		67.30	
dividends per share	17.70		26.50		30.50		36.50	

Amec Balance Sheet

	31 Dec 2009 (GBP)		31 Dec 2010 (GBP)		31 Dec 2011 (GBP)		31 Dec 2012 (GBP)	
LIABILITIES Creditors (short) Creditors (long & other) Total Equity ASSETS Intangibles Fixed assets & Fixed investment Current assets (other) & Stocks & Debtors Cash & Equivalents Total Negative Equity	1,935.40	1,935.40	2,263.30	2,263.30	2,455.00	2,455.00	2,518.00	2,518.00

	31 Dec 2009 (GBP)		31 Dec 2010 (GBP)		31 Dec 2011 (GBP)		31 Dec 2012 (GBP)	
ASSETS								
fixed assets	44.10	2.28%	31.90	1.41%	35.00	1.43%	43.00	1.71% m
intangibles	454.40	23.48%	621.30	27.45%	848.00	34.54%	969.00	38.48% m
fixed investments	157.90	8.16%	165.50	7.31%	45.00	1.83%	134.00	5.32% m
current assets - other	-	-%	-	-%	-	-%	-	-% m
stocks	5.40	0.28%	1.40	0.06%	4.00	0.16%	4.00	0.16% m
debtors	661.60	34.18%	899.50	39.74%	1,030.00	41.96%	1,110.00	44.08% m
cash & securities	612.00	31.62%	543.70	24.02%	493.00	20.08%	258.00	10.25% m
TOTAL	1,935.40	100%	2,263.30	100%	2,455.00	100%	2,518.00	100% m
LIABILITIES								
creditors - short	659.20	34.06%	746.20	32.97%	828.00	33.73%	1,151.00	45.71% m
creditors - long	249.90	12.91%	242.10	10.70%	253.00	10.31%	284.00	11.28% m
creditors - other	-	-%	-	-%	-	-%	-	-% m
subordinated loans	-	-%	-	-%	-	-%	-	-% m
insurance funds	-	-%	-	-%	-	-%	-	-% m

I look at cash this way. If a company is cheap and in trouble but has a cash war chest, it can keep itself going and away from the pillagers that prey on failing companies. Cash gives a company flexibility and time. Cash is the power to survive and overcome.

Looking deeper at a company, a steadily growing pile of cash will indicate that the business is actually growing or at least improving. Growing cash is a good indication that the business is going well.

Back to Vodafone, for an example of a company with cash pouring in:

Vodafone Fundamentals

	31 Mar 2010 (GBP)		31 Mar 2011 (GBP)		31 Mar 2012 (GBP)		31 Mar 2013 (GBP)	
turnover	44,472.00	100.00%	45,884.00	100.00%	46,417.00	100.00%	44,445.00	100.00% m
pre tax profit	8,674.00	19.50%	9,498.00	20.70%	9,549.00	20.57%	3,255.00	7.32% m
attributable profit	8,645.00	19.44%	7,968.00	17.37%	6,957.00	14.99%	429.00	0.97% m
retained profit	4,506.00	10.13%	3,500.00	7.63%	314.00	0.68%	-4,377.00	-9.85% m
eps - basic	16.44		15.20		13.74		0.87	
eps - diluted	16.36		15.11		13.65		0.87	
dividends per share	8.31		8.90		9.52		10.19	

Vodafone Balance Sheet

	31 Mar 2010 (GBP)		31 Mar 2011 (GBP)		31 Mar 2012 (GBP)		31 Mar 2013 (GBP)	
LIABILITIES								
Creditors (short)	156.99k	156.98k	151.22k	151.22k	139.58k	139.58k	142.70k	142.70k
Creditors (long & other)								
Total Equity								
ASSETS								
Intangibles								
Fixed assets & Fixed investment								
Current assets (other) & Stocks & Debtors								
Cash & Equivalents								
Total Negative Equity								

	31 Mar 2010 (GBP)		31 Mar 2011 (GBP)		31 Mar 2012 (GBP)		31 Mar 2013 (GBP)	
ASSETS								
fixed assets	20,642.00	13.15%	20,181.00	13.35%	18,655.00	13.37%	20,331.00	14.25% m
intangibles	74,268.00	47.30%	68,558.00	45.34%	59,514.00	42.64%	52,397.00	36.72% m
fixed investments	47,866.00	30.49%	40,257.00	26.62%	37,263.00	26.69%	44,811.00	31.40% m
current assets - other	-	-%	-	-%	-	-%	-	-% m
stocks	433.00	0.28%	537.00	0.36%	486.00	0.35%	450.00	0.32% m
debtors	9,363.00	5.96%	15,435.00	10.21%	16,530.00	11.84%	17,086.00	11.97% m
cash & securities	4,423.00	2.82%	6,252.00	4.13%	7,138.00	5.11%	7,623.00	5.34% m
TOTAL	156,985.00	100%	151,220.00	100%	139,576.00	100%	142,698.00	100% m

While accountants can magic profits in and out of existence they can't hide cash. As such cash is solid evidence that things might be just fine behind the scenes. This might not be in question with a massive blue chip like Vodafone, but for an obscure company a fraction of its size that might not be clear at all from much of the accounts.

In hard times cash is king and companies that have halved in value are in a difficult spot. This is why they are cheap. It is their capacity to turn things around that makes them good investments and for that they need cash in the bank.

Recap Criteria 5

The company should have more than £10 million of cash in the bank. The bigger the company the more it should have, but a £10 million base line is a solid cut off. You can't have too much cash, so there is no upper limit. Again you can tweak the level down but under £1 million and you can safely conclude the company has no cash left.

Financial Criteria 6: Sales to Market Cap

It is sometimes said it is easy to sell lots of stuff but it is hard to make a profit. The latter half is certainly true but the first half of the assertion is utter nonsense. It is hard to sell lots of anything. That is why salesmen are so well paid—selling is hard. Anyone who has actually tried selling will tell you it's a tricky business.

'Sales' is also the top line of a business, the first process that drives the whole machine of a company. You can dispense with lots of things in a business and it will keep going. You could tear out the plumbing and businesses would still carry on. However, stop sales and most companies would pack up and close in days.

As such, the sales of a company are vital. The importance of sales is also underestimated, especially in snotty Britain. This makes sales another good criterion to go checking into.

Clearly if a company has huge sales yet has a low market cap then that is good news if we are looking for a cheap share. There are a few ways this works.

For instance, say you have two companies that do very much the same thing. Let's use the example of mobile phones. If the companies sell roughly the same amount yet are valued wildly differently, as far as their market cap is concerned, something might be wrong with the company with the low valuation, or that company may be cheap.

A good example of this was Orange, when it was listed in London. It was in essence a very similar company to Vodafone yet the company's worth was much less when compared pound for pound in sales against VOD, as investors call it.

These companies were at the time fighting for market share so it was hard to see exactly how loss-making or profitable they really were, but the sales were clear.

Orange was valued at a fraction of Vodafone per pound of sales. That didn't last because French Telecom snapped them up. They wanted those sales and that business was cheap, so they took it over. If two companies are very similar except their market cap/sales ratio are very different, it is a positive sign for the lowly valued company that it is cheap, as it is selling a lot more per unit of market cap than the similar but more highly regarded business.

Another reason why this is a good thing to study is that some companies get so out of fashion you can buy their whole business for a few days of sales. If that company is not about to go broke it is clear the business is cheap.

The reason is that if the company gets taken over, the new owner can simply extend credit payment terms a few days and cover the purchase cost of the company with cash flow. That is a very tempting prospect for corporate raiders.

This is exactly the sort of trick that 'private equity'—companies that buy up cheap public companies—get up to and many a 'private equity' takeover has paid a value investor a handsome premium.

Likewise a new owner can—and they do—send all their creditors a 5% debit note with a letter saying "please credit us this or else we will no longer buy anything else from you" and in this way they hope to pay for the business in one fell swoop.

This was the type of thing that happened to Arcadia, a company that went from 30p a share to 400p a share in a matter of months and yet still paid out its new owner hundreds of million in dividends when it was taken over at that elevated price. At one stage a few days of sales could buy the business and then the price rocketed and in the end 'private equity' gobbled the company up.

If a business can sell a lot of its products, it is likely to be well run. While all sorts of things can go wrong with a company, the more a company sells as a ratio to its market cap the more likely it is to be cheap.

An average company is valued at £1 of market cap to £1 of sales. That is a good benchmark. Some companies are worth ten times sales, some are worth 0.1 times sales; the difference of course between those two companies is that one company's sales are worth a hundred times more than another's.

It is clearly odd that a pound of sales of one company can be worth a hundred times more than another and this is the basis of why we look at this number. It might not be odd, it might just be wrong.

The values we are looking for are companies with a sales to market capitalisation ratio of less than 1. This means a company's sales total more than the company can be bought for.

To start with we can cut out any company that is worth more than half its sales, or has a ratio greater than 0.5. We don't need to be gentle; there are plenty of companies that will survive this guillotine.

A company worth only .1 or 10% of sales is fine too; there are a lot of companies down there and they can come roaring back. As such we should initially set the cut off at 0.5, because value investment style companies sell lots of product but are not considered highly because of it.

Recap Criteria 6

Exclude companies that are valued at less than half of their sales.

Financial Criteria 7: Equity

Equity is a term which has two meanings in investment. It means shares—a share is equity—and it means how much money the shares have a hold over.

In this judgement criterion, equity means the latter; how much money is left for the shareholders if everyone was paid off.

Below is a diagram of a company's balance sheet. The left column is liabilities and the right is assets.

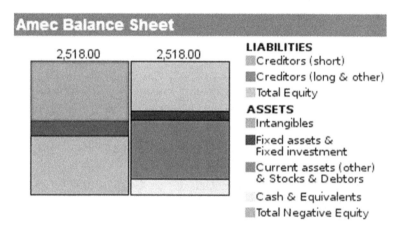

You can see they balance. The balancing item between assets and liabilities is equity.

That is because shares are a liability so that if you paid off all creditors and other liabilities with assets, the money left over would go to the equity shareholders.

Equity is the chunk at the bottom left. This example has a nice fat lump of equity.

If the company didn't have enough assets to pay off its creditors there would be nothing left for the equity portion. So the less equity there is, the less sound a company is. Some companies have minus equity, or as most understand this idea, 'negative equity.'

This means they do not have enough money today to pay off everyone. This makes their finances very shaky. Happily they owe banks and have bonds and these aren't going to be called on to be paid off immediately; or so it is hoped. If a company is making good profits it can roll these debts and carry on paying their debts down. This often happens.

However if a company is up the creek this situation can bring down the house. As such equity is a good place to check. The more the better.

But there is another wrinkle: assets called intangibles. These are assets which are extremely vague and really the only reason they are tracked is to stop many companies from avoiding tax.

No one ever bought dinner with an intangible asset, I wonder if anyone ever paid a debt with one. Why? Because they are intangible—you can't see, smell or touch them.

If, however, you buy my software company for a lot of money and there are no buildings, machines etc., then the balance you appeared to pay for that floppy disk of computer code goes in the books as intangible. That can be correct, but the same reasoning can value all kinds of crud as an intangible asset.

Intangibles are slippery and many a mountain of them vanishes in good time. This means you should ignore intangibles when you look at a company and then judge whether it can pay its bills or not. A company with little equity and a lot of intangibles may well be a dead duck. So keep an eye on intangibles when making your final selection.

Here is an example of a balance sheet of a company that went horribly bust: Connaught.

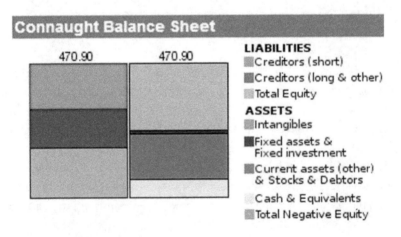

If you take out the intangibles of this council house drain cleaning company then you will see it owes more than it has in assets to pay them off. There was more perhaps to this company than drain cleaning but when the cold winds of the credit crunch blew it quickly got flushed down the pan. If it had more equity and less intangibles it would be trading today.

Again this is simply a way of running another test of the companies you are looking to buy. It is another way to kick the tires.

Recap Criteria 7

Discard all companies with negative equity.

No-Nos!

Companies can look great but in reality there is something nasty going on. The company can fit all the criteria nicely, have a marvellous balance sheet, but still you want to invoke a special rule and say no thanks. Here are mine. You should look to develop your own over time. Investing is a game of skill and like all skill-based activities, skill will develop with practice. The more skill you develop, the bigger your returns will be.

No-No 1: Family Firms

Blood is thicker than water and family firms carry a risk that business is not for the benefit solely of shareholders but for the benefit of the family.

The chairman's son may be a bright guy, but it would be incredible that he was absolutely the right and best executive in the world to run the company. Who could possibly imagine that the fact he is the son of the boss wasn't a big factor in his hiring?

There is nothing wrong with this per se, good luck to them, because we can see the relationship upfront and decide accordingly whether to invest. This is how the market should work, not though edict but through transparency. That doesn't mean, however, that family inheritance in the governance of a PLC is a good thing.

When companies don't act in the sole interest of their shareholders, investors should beware. Over time I have noticed many family businesses fail on the markets, to be bought back for a song by the family shareholders. This makes them as a whole group dangerous to your wealth. I apologise to scrupulous family firms, I'm sure there are paragons, but an overall heightened risk means I throw every single one of them out of my stock picking universe. I'm surely wrong about some of them and I'm sure it's my loss, but as a group their specialness disqualifies family firms out of hand. Someone else is welcome to the gold nugget that gets away.

Apart from the risk of close family ties to outsiders the opposite can also be a big danger. Families fall out and then all sorts of internecine actions take place which can destroy a business.

The conflict of interest inherent in family firms means that I will exclude a value stock which is family run.

When it comes to family, family comes first, which is how it should be; however, I don't want to be on the outside of that arrangement when investing.

No-No 2: Government Footballs

Governments are unpredictable things. Their policies are unstable and they are run by people who care little for economics or business. Governments care about politics and will warp, destroy and generally mess up anything in business they touch. Governments don't care about profits, they care about taxation. Politicians don't care about profits either; they care about votes and getting good press.

If you have a business and politicians think they can get votes closing you down, they will close you down.

You might be providing a vital service, or be trying to, you might be employing thousands, but if there are votes in it to stomp on your business they will do it without a thought.

Cover a mountain with giant windmills at uneconomic prices, no problems.

Have a coal mine which might produce energy for everyone cheaply but is sited near a pretty village with important votes or with some rare amphibians nearby, forget even trying to get going.

Political footballs are always utterly vulnerable to disaster originating from the government and political system. Once a share is ensnared in politics it is immediately poised on the edge of doom.

Of course there are plenty of examples but a notable one to research is Railtrack; I could write a separate book on that case and I'm sure someone has. Companies get horribly mashed up by being too close to government time and again.

If a company is a political football, just say no.

For example, it takes a lot of nerve to hold a nationalised bank like Lloyds, being aware that it only takes a single bad decision from government to kill the value of that company. This is ironic as I hold this company as of January 2012 and only time will tell if this rule-breaking position will bite me. If you are going to break rules a huge amount of consideration is required, if only to have your excuses lined up when things go south.

No-No 3: Financial Restatements

If you own shares in a company that restates its financial figures revealing a hole in its accounts, sell it. Only if it is trivial should you not bail immediately.

Certainly do not buy the share that reveals accounting errors of any material kind unless it happened a long time ago and the management has changed significantly. Even then be very careful.

Many companies that restate their figures promptly go bust.

It shouldn't be the case that there is any skulduggery on the stock market but it is fair to say not many weeks go by without some scandal or other cropping up.

This is exacerbated by modern accounting that produces company accounts far removed from a financial reality we would recognise as a member of the public. The arcane nature of accounts means that all sorts of nonsense can go on in the shadows and then be buried away out of sight.

An investor is reliant on the company's auditors and the honesty of a company's directors to make investments. If these barriers are breached then the investor has nothing to go on. As such if a company reveals a significant inaccuracy in its past accounts, unless of course miracles of miracles the company has done better than it thought, sell the shares immediately or refuse to buy any if that is the reason it is 'cheap.' There are plenty of cheap companies and there is no need to risk good money on dodgy accounting.

No-No 4: Legal Outcomes

Don't buy companies that are relying on the outcome of a big court case to change their fortunes.

The law is not known as a good business model for anyone but lawyers and funnily enough there aren't any/many lawyers listed on the stock market.

This doesn't stop certain companies that look cheap on paper to actually be relying on some kind of pay-out in court to keep them going. Sometimes this can pay off, but it's simply not worth investing in the faint hope. Companies mired in litigation do not often prosper; the more unlikely the court action or remote from a decent jurisdiction the case is, the worse the prospects.

This kind of thing often affects mining companies. As soon as they hit pay dirt someone tries to muscle in using the 'interesting' local law system to try and grab the winnings. This is a situation that a value investor doesn't need or want to invest in.

Let the lawyers make their money and steer well clear.

Value Investing: How To Do It In Practice

Step 1: Build a Portfolio

You have to be prepared to lose money when you invest. At least to begin with.

This is just a function of the process. There are costs that can put you 2-3% behind and then there is the fact that there is no chance of buying at the absolute bottom of any company's share price.

Roughly speaking, for every share you buy only one in ten will not go lower and never go lower than where you buy it at. If you could accurately pick the bottom for stocks you would quickly be the richest man in the world. Value investing can make you the richest person in the world—like Mr Buffett—but it takes a lot longer than it would if you could judge the bottom of the market for a share.

This is why Buffett doesn't seem to care when he buys a stock for $18 only to see it fall to $6: because in the long run it will be $100 and maybe well more than that. You can't pick the bottom or the top of the market, you just need to buy cheap shares and then sell them when the stock has gone up and is not cheap anymore.

Over time you will get into profit.

You will get into profit quickly in a bull market and slowly in a bear market. The thing to remember is you will be right and you will be wrong, you will be unlucky and you will be lucky. You have a sensible system not a crystal ball, so you will win some and you will lose some and the result will be a good profit.

You really do not want to buy too few companies with your money, you want to buy a group of different companies using the same selection system so that the profits are protected from luck and get smoothed.

Buying a bunch of stocks is called a portfolio and it gives you diversification. The more stocks you have the more diversified you are.

You know about not having all your eggs in one basket. That is what portfolio diversification is all about.

Imagine you are really good at a game of chance, for example roulette.

Let's say you play black and red and amazingly you can get it right two times out of three, so you should make a fortune. However, if you put all your money on each go you would lose all your money soon enough and be broke. Betting like that, you'd never get rich. This in its simplest form is why you don't put your money in too few shares. If you put all your money eggs in one basket case share you can be wiped out.

A portfolio protects you.

Also funny things happen when you have more than a few of anything.

Take dice.

If you throw one die, you will get a score between 1 and 6 and the number of times the numbers 1, 2, 3, 4, 5, and 6 come up will be even across the whole range.

Now take two dice and you will find 7 will be the result more often than 1 or 12. Take a thousand dice and the result of throwing them will very often be in a narrow range of the possible total outcomes. The number of dice involved smooth out the result.

Do this with a million dice and the likelihood of a small range of results will increase even more. The more dice you throw the more likely the result will be the same each time and of course the average result for each dice will become more stable too.

Shares can be like dice; a bunch of them will smooth out the results of your selection.

It makes your results smooth and clear. There is no wondering if things are going too well or too badly, because a portfolio spreads your risk and makes your profits smooth.

A portfolio is a good way to take the stress out of investing. Who needs more stress?

I track my portfolio using ADVFN's excellent portfolio charting tool. I can see the day-to-day total profit change and gauge if things are going my way over the long term. It also lets me track defunct portfolios I may have closed out on long ago and it lets me create theoretical portfolios to see how an investment idea turns out.

Why not put all those tips into a portfolio and see how you get on— who knows, maybe someone is a hot tipster after all.

Below is an example of a portfolio of companies I thought might get taken over, which I built in theory using the ADVFN portfolio tool, just before the roof caved in during the credit crunch.

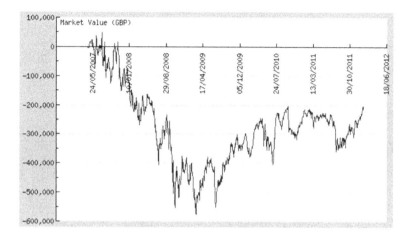

With this image I can see a few obvious lessons staring me in the face. Takeover targets get hit hard in a crash, rally hard and if you have OK stocks and you are prepared to hang onto them for a long time then things tend to recover . . . But that's not the point. The point is that the behaviour of a portfolio gives you an insight to how in the medium term you are doing and if you are doing your investing correctly.

This chart tells me that buying takeover targets in a bull market can be a risky game. So that's one thing I'm not planning to do.

Step 2: Portfolio Size

To be a sensible value investor you need thirty shares in your portfolio.

You might say, hold on a moment, that means I need a big slug of cash to get going and I don't have that much money.

That is OK.

Let's say you buy £1,000 of a share that you decide to invest in after running all the criteria and rules. £1,000 is a sensible quantity.

You will therefore need £30,000 to buy a proper portfolio.

But you don't have £30,000 right now. What are you to do?

All is not lost as investing is going to be a long term project.

You can start with one share and save for the next.

As the months pass, even years, you will expand your portfolio towards the thirty target.

As you do so your results will smooth out. As long as you keep the size of your share buys in any company to an initial purchase of £1,000 each time, your profits and further investments will get you to a thirty share portfolio. As you progress the benefits of a portfolio will increasingly kick in.

A purist would sell down any share that does very well, so if you were lucky enough to double your money in one share, you would sell half and find another share. However you shouldn't obsess about this kind of thing too much. It will be a nice problem to have at some point but it's really better to keep things simple.

Step 3: Making a Selection

Let's say you are just getting started.

First things first, do you own shares now?

If you do, get them into your brokerage account.

Then examine them. If you don't know why you own them or why you bought them, or exactly why you are keeping them, then sell them. Never own an orphan stock.

For fresh beginners, prime your account with some cash.

Decide your investment 'clip.'

This is the amount you buy of a share you want to add to the portfolio. It might be less than £1,000 a share but £1,000 is really a good minimum. Definitely do not invest less than £500.

Why? Because the costs of buying and selling usually have a fixed minimum and this will eat too much of the profit percentage you make if you own too small an amount of shares.

So you are ready to buy your first share.

Firstly you must trawl through a sea of stocks to select the best ten shares you can find that fit the criteria.

Here's how you do that using FilterX on ADVFN as an example.

To use FilterX you need to register with ADVFN. Go to the website at http://www.advfn.com and click the FREE MEMBERSHIP button to register. FilterX is free to use and ADVFN charges you nothing to use it, or for that matter any number of its smart tools. It can do this by carrying adverts from stock brokers, etc. It also has super sophisticated products for keen traders who need their price information in real time and who need to see into the inner working of how prices are formed, using tools such as Level 2.

Meanwhile value investors can use FilterX for free, no charge, nada. They can also go to a section called Financials where every company on the London stock exchange has all its balance sheets and results laid bare. This sort of information used to cost thousands of pounds, but the data is free on ADVFN.

To use FilterX, you log onto ADVFN, click on FINANCIALS and then FilterX.

You build a filter using the financial criteria, discarding all companies that don't fit them.

To construct your new filter, click START FILTERX. You get a long list of all companies on the exchange, which you can start to prune down to those you are interested in.

Start by adding columns for all the criteria you are going to use, by selecting from the three dropdown boxes. The columns I add are:

- P/E ratio (from Key Figures)
- Dividend yield (from Key Figures)
- Cash (from Fundamentals)
- Price/sales (from Deeper Analysis)
- % 1 year (from Key Figures)
- % 3 year(from Key Figures)
- Equity (from Fundamentals)
- Bid (from Key Figures)

So it looks like this:

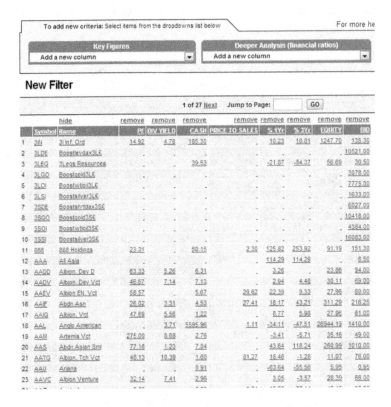

Now you start to define the criteria you want to use to discard companies. Click on the P/E number for any company and you will go automatically to a screen that lets you filter out ranges of P/E:

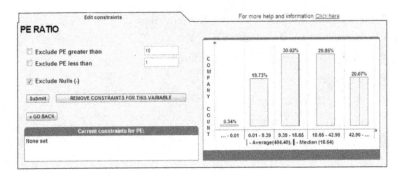

Interestingly the tool tells us that a 14 is the most common P/E on the London market. By picking our criteria to filter the UK market, 1,800 companies are immediately removed. We now have roughly 400 to look at.

At this stage I'm going to remove all companies that aren't trading by filtering out all companies who do not have a 'bid' price, i.e. you can't buy or sell shares in. These companies may have been stopped from trading or have recently gone bust. This makes scanning the columns easier.

Now I'm going to zap all companies not paying enough dividends. Gone are all companies paying more than 10% a year or less than 3%. I now have 135 companies to look at.

I'm now going to knock out all companies which are worth more than half their sales. I note after the last two culls the remaining companies have 'sales to market cap' on average of 1.5 but the most common value is just above half times sales, near the zone I want.

I'm now down to 62 companies in the list.

New Filter

[BID Excluded: Nulls (-)] [PE < 10] [PE > 1] [PE Excluded: Nulls (-)] [DIV YIELD < 10] [DIV YIELD E

			hide	remove	remove	remove		remove	remove	remove	remove	remove
	Symbol	Name	PE	DIV YIELD	CASH	PRICE TO SALES		% 1Yr	% 3Yr	EQUITY	BID
1	ABM	Albemarle & BD	4.68	9.55	5.08	0.52		-50.56	-40.13	80.29	128.00
2	AEC	Aec Educ.	9.59	2.86	3.81	0.16		-36.36	-60.00	8.05	6.50
3	AGA	Aga Rangemaster	8.53	2.23	21.00	0.24		14.05	-3.12	141.20	84.50
4	AGD	Anglogold Ash	8.59	1.26	588.27	1.10		201.68	301.68	3365.33	1025.00
5	AML	Amlin	7.72	6.21	190.60	0.97		15.59	-0.10	1491.40	385.80
6	BEZ	Beazley	8.27	3.72	391.67	1.19		62.61	83.47	745.62	222.80
7	BISI	Bisichi Mining	9.17	3.56	1.80	0.33		7.14	-41.56	17.76	110.00
8	BLT	Bhp Billiton	9.76	3.97	3044.10	0.87		-1.75	-9.53	42713.52	1798.00
9	BMT	Braimean/V	9.42	1.46	1.75	1.07		8.12	491.67	5.94	515.00
10	BVM	Beloravium Tech	8.33	3.64	1.61	0.32		-60.71	.	11.13	2.50
11	C21	21ST Cent Tech	6.72	7.18	1.71	0.65		-45.07	44.44	8.00	9.50
12	CCT	Character Grp	4.95	5.22	5.91	0.38		-11.23	-6.64	9.98	123.00
13	CFYN	Caffyns	8.37	3.08	1.16	0.07		.	-13.33	15.31	370.00
14	CGL	Catlin Grp	8.56	6.14	1522.37	0.57		14.31	30.52	2161.10	480.10
15	CLDN	Caledonia Inv.	5.13	2.58	116.20	3.14		34.66	11.34	1275.80	1833.00
16	CLIG	City Lon Inv	7.31	9.72	5.40	1.94		-23.53	-14.68	15.29	244.25
17	CLLN	Carillion	7.08	6.55	657.10	0.26		-3.97	-19.94	1009.50	263.40
18	CMH	Chamberlin	9.00	3.61	.	0.17		-42.68	31.39	8.29	88.00
19	CMX	Catalyst Media	7.13	6.36	1.46	1216.41		89.23	33.33	36.09	107.00
20	CNKS	Cenkos Sec	7.44	8.33	22.27	1.27		69.81	-10.45	22.23	88.00
21	COST	Costain Grp.	6.82	4.25	107.40	0.18		21.93	21.63	31.80	251.75
22	CPW	Carphone	1.46	2.06	102.70	197.63		74.37	26.86	708.00	243.50

At this stage I'm going to add a column for market cap value to the filter, as the size of the business might sway me later.

Now we are going to hack away companies with less than £10 million in cash. We now have just 31 companies.

New Filter
[BID Excluded: Nulls (-)] [PE < 10] [PE > 1] [PE Excluded: Nulls (-)] [DIV YIELD < 10] [DIV YIELD Excluded: Nu CAP(M) Excluded: Nulls (-)]

1 of 1   Jump to Page: [   ] [GO]

	Symbol	Name	PE	DIV YIELD	CASH	PRICE TO SALES	% 1Yr	% 3Yr	EQUITY	BID	MKT CAP(M)
1	RDSA	Rds A	7.82	6.14	11414.68	0.23	-0.68	14.18	116870.96	2113.50	80279.20
2	RDSB	Rds B	8.07	4.85	11414.68	0.19	-0.80	22.88	116870.96	2183.00	55744.17
3	BLT	Bhp Billiton	9.76	3.97	3044.10	0.87	-1.75	-9.53	42713.52	1798.00	37985.61
4	OML	Old Mutual	7.52	3.74	3863.00	0.46	22.42	63.01	9798.00	187.20	9170.88
5	FQM	First Quantum	4.47	1.02	190.14	3.46	-10.21	24.27	3619.10	1047.00	6286.50
6	AGD	Anglogold Ash	8.59	1.29	588.27	1.10	301.68	301.68	3365.33	1025.00	4508.92
7	DGO	Dragon Oil	7.94	3.06	171.06	4.17	9.63	39.30	1759.47	602.00	2964.63
8	AML	Amin	7.72	6.21	190.60	0.97	15.59	-0.10	1491.40	385.80	1931.67
9	GPOR	GR Portland	9.73	1.57	6.30	27.31	43.42	88.25	1537.70	547.00	1884.72
10	LAD	Ladbrokes	9.66	4.39	19.40	1.72	18.53	49.67	422.30	202.60	1861.14
11	ICP	Int.Cap.Grp	9.43	4.23	159.30	4.13	74.33	71.47	1450.70	449.30	1806.05
12	CGL	Catlin Grp	8.58	6.14	1522.37	0.57	14.31	30.52	2161.10	480.10	1737.78
13	PHNX	Phoenix Grp(DI)	2.89	7.29	9028.00	1.25	42.08	2.75	2392.00	653.50	1470.15
14	LRE	Lancashire	8.36	1.18	182.02	3.27	1.17	58.49	853.73	781.00	1286.77
15	CPW	Carphone	1.46	2.06	102.70	197.63	74.37	26.86	708.00	243.50	1264.86
16	BEZ	Beazley	8.27	3.72	381.87	1.19	62.61	83.47	745.62	222.80	1162.31
17	HTG	Hunting	8.82	2.37	101.70	1.39	0.19	69.46	813.80	779.50	1149.86
18	CLLN	Carillion	7.06	6.55	657.10	0.26	-3.97	-19.94	1009.50	263.40	1133.29
19	DEB	Debenhams	9.01	3.40	44.00	0.50	10.24	49.53	661.00	88.15	1105.43
20	ELM	Elementis	9.94	2.03	63.10	1.43	19.47	299.32	482.20	235.50	1079.66
21	CLDN	Caledonia Inv.	5.13	2.58	116.20	3.14	34.68	11.34	1275.90	1833.00	1021.39
22	FXPO	Ferrexpo	6.59	2.65	367.09	1.03	-26.63	-47.61	966.09	153.40	903.54
23	MGAM	Morgan Advanced	9.93	3.62	80.00	0.78	-1.99	39.68	271.80	276.00	786.30
24	HOC	Hochschild	6.56	1.85	403.69	1.01	-57.47	-36.69	784.29	208.30	641.75
25	IRV	Interserve	3.71	4.19	76.80	0.27	62.79	126.13	330.80	489.00	630.04
26	WKP	Workspace Grp.	7.68	2.36	11.80	8.53	76.34	92.52	500.40	408.80	592.93
27	NMC	Nmc Health	8.19	1.30	23.75	1.19	57.69	50.10	331.60	315.20	585.33
28	UTG	Unite Group	4.65	1.12	75.40	2.66	83.69	85.75	533.70	354.90	571.32
29	JHD	James Halstead	9.16	5.92	38.70	2.47	3.94	71.59	94.34	270.00	558.60
30	KIE	Kier Group	8.19	5.65	159.10	0.22	-6.93	15.99	154.20	1169.00	465.40
31	FBH	F.B.D.Hldgs	9.52	3.06	25.71	1.19	69.33	84.00	244.66	13.65	464.57

Here they are sorted by market capitalisation. It is not surprising that I own a fair few of these stocks.

Now if I knock out anything that hasn't halved in either the last year or the last three years, I'm only left with two stocks. I own them both.

I don't need all the stocks I own to stay in this range; it is only a signal to consider buying in. Selling we will consider later.

The beauty of the system is even though we refine down to two stocks, both in this case solid educational technology companies, I can see a whole bunch of what is known as 'edge cases,' shares not totally fitting the criteria but nonetheless interesting.

Looking into these firms further will highlight future candidates or perhaps a compelling candidate to take to the next round or to just keep an eye on.

At this point we should select the ten most interesting companies on this list.

Draw up a spreadsheet or write them down on a scrap of paper.

Then go to their quote on ADVFN and find their news. Read the last couple of years of the interim and final accounts statements. Look for directors buying. Check the balance sheet to make sure it has equity and for anything that looks odd. Then score each criterion out of ten, using your judgement to rate the companies for their different values like this:

	A	B	C	D	E	F	G	H	I
1		P/E	Dividend	Cash	Price/sales	Fall	Equity	Directors buys	Total
2	Company A	7	8	2	4	4	3	8	36
3	Company B	3	6	3	5	5	8	9	39
4	Company C	5	9	7	9	6	6	1	43
5	Company D	2	6	8	8	5	5	3	37
6	Company E	4	3	4	5	4	6	0	26

Company C would be your winner and an investor would buy that. If you are careful you will surf the web and check out the company's website etc. before making the final decision.

You can of course refine this process a million ways and in fact in time you will. I very rarely need to use a filter these days because I'm running the stock picking screen in my head every time I look at a share. Given time you will too.

As the weeks roll by you will soon have value stocks in a portfolio that will over time give you a good return and you can repeat the process every few weeks to see if anything new has popped up. You can play with the filter making the criteria tougher or gentler as you go. This framework will soon get you familiar with a lot of shares and keep you on a sensible path.

Step 4: Buying Shares

Coming up with lists of likely shares to put in your portfolio is no good at all if you don't actually put all that theory into practice, and buy some shares.

For that you need a broker—a company that sorts out the buying and selling of shares and charges you for that service. You open an account with a broker, send them some money, and then buy and sell stocks.

Opening a brokerage account has got harder over the years. We are probably all familiar by now with having to prove who we are when opening bank accounts and such like, and like a bank, the broker will want utility bills and copies of passports or drivers licences with mug shots. Allow yourself a couple of weeks messing around to get an account set up. It shouldn't take that long, but it's best to have your account set up well in advance because if you want to buy a share and you don't have your account open you will be stuck.

There are telephone brokers and online brokers – some companies offer both services.

An example of an online broker is The Share Centre (http://www.share.com).

I am happy to endorse this company.

A Few Other Issues

Issue 1: Investing Costs

Trading in and out of stocks is very expensive indeed. Do it too much and you will burn through your cash and end up with nothing. Trading without a very, very, good reason is trading randomly. Random trading will make you win half the time and lose half the time, minus the cost of trading. You will note this will doom you to blow all your money. Investing is not random and therefore you will earn profits. Trading randomly only makes your broker rich.

Churning your investments can bleed you white. Don't do it!

The average period I hold a value investment is about eighteen months. It can be a few days if I get excessively lucky, it can be for three years if I see the opportunity too far off. It averages out. It also keeps costs low.

Turning my portfolio over every eighteen months means my costs are less than 1% of my capital a year. If I turned it over twice as fast my costs would double. If I went faster my costs would begin to become prohibitive. Value investing is cheap and that is one of the reasons it succeeds.

Issue 2: Charts

Charts can only tell you the future if you have spotted something no one else has. If you read about a chart technique in an old popular book on charts, the scheme will not work. There is an army of maths PhDs looking at the numbers behind charts who have huge computers churning through the data to try and predict the future. As such you can happily give up trying yourself, unless you are a maths PhD with a large computer.

What you can do is use charts to predict the past. Everyone can predict the past but the past can be reassuring and informative. It can tell you about the story you are buying into but don't hope to get too much of an insight about tomorrow. Of course I don't follow my own advice on this, but that is only human nature. There is no harm in trying to predict the future from the charts but the reality is if you could do it reliably you'd make all the money in the world, like Jim Evans, the hero of my thrillers The Armageddon Trade, The Twain Maxim and Kusanagi.

By all means get acquainted with technical analysis, but remember, chart schemes of the past have already been picked over a million times and pre-empted to death.

Issue 3: Selling

Classically when you see a 30% profit on a value investment you are meant to sell. You won't go far wrong doing this. Occasionally a stock you have held will run a lot further and it is frustrating to sell out early on a stock that then goes up three, four, even ten times. There is probably no way of deciding how far to run your profits, but you will often be rewarded by not being greedy. I tend to sell at around 30% but if there has just been a crash and stocks have fallen massively, I will cling on for a jumbo rise. After a crash you hold on till normality resumes and then sell.

However, a share can go up a long way and then fall to nothing; there isn't a good way of knowing. Our idea is to buy when a share is cheap and sell it when it is NOT cheap. Anything beyond this is not value investing, it's gambling. As your skill develops you will get the hang of it or at least feel you have. When a share you hold has gone up enough to seem similar to the random herd of companies, then it's most likely a good time to sell it. A 30% rise will often achieve that goal.

A few other ideas that appear to work for selling are:

- Sell when the share jumps on good news.
- Sell on any big rally that seems to have no reason, but perhaps wait a day or two after the rally ends.
- Sell when the share is back or nearly back to a similar valuation ratio to shares in the same sector.
- Sell when a share has recovered to a level it has traded at comfortably in the past, which represents a return to normality.
- Sell if an accounting irregularity appears.
- Sell if you've forgotten why the stock is in the portfolio in the first place. (This can happen sometimes.)
- Sell when a takeover has been mooted as possible in an RNS but not yet confirmed. Perhaps wait a day or two first. This is infuriating when the company jumps two months later but many 'almost takeovers' evaporate.
- Sell when the newspapers start saying, "Buy this stock," after the share has already risen from the grave.
- Sell if you conclude the CEO is bonkers or a crook.

Issue 4: Compounding

If you can make 25% a year you will increase your capital by ten times in a decade. That means a hundred times in twenty years and a thousand times in thirty years and of course ten thousand in forty years.

This is why Mr Buffett has so much money. It is also why it is hard to make 25% every year.

It also shows how even with rates like 10%, small amounts of money compounded can turn into big piles of cash given enough time.

This is why it's good to start young.

Compounding is the key to this game and keeping costs down and keeping profits under tax shelters like ISAs is so important. Value investing is a winning game and winnings must be protected and nurtured.

If you are a Brit, start out with an ISA and build your portfolio there. Think of it as at least a five year project, better still ten or twenty years. After a few years you will not be the first person to be shocked about how much capital you have built up. Try not to use the result to build a new kitchen or move house, the best is yet to come. The bigger your portfolio gets, the bigger the impact on your wealth. Do a spreadsheet and build an investment plan that folds a growth figure into it like the one below. Then see the results over ten, twenty or thirty years. It will make your eyes bug out.

	A	B	C	D	E	F
1	Year	Money in per yr	"@7%"	"@10%"	"@15%"	"@25%"
2	1	1,000	1,070	1,100	1,150	1,250
3	2	1,000	2,215	2,310	2,473	2,813
4	3	1,000	3,440	3,641	3,993	4,766
5	4	1,000	4,751	5,105	5,742	7,207
6	5	1,000	6,153	6,716	7,754	10,259
7	6	1,000	7,654	8,487	10,067	14,073
8	7	1,000	9,260	10,436	12,727	18,842
9	8	1,000	10,978	12,579	15,786	24,802
10	9	1,000	12,816	14,937	19,304	32,253
11	10	1,000	14,784	17,531	23,349	41,566
12	11	1,000	16,888	20,384	28,002	53,208
13	12	1,000	19,141	23,523	33,352	67,760
14	13	1,000	21,550	26,975	39,505	85,949
15	14	1,000	24,129	30,772	46,580	108,687
16	15	1,000	26,888	34,950	54,717	137,109
17	16	1,000	29,840	39,545	64,075	172,636
18	17	1,000	32,999	44,599	74,836	217,045
19	18	1,000	36,379	50,159	87,212	272,556
20	19	1,000	39,995	56,275	101,444	341,945
21	20	1,000	43,865	63,002	117,810	428,681
22	21	1,000	48,006	70,403	136,632	537,101
23	22	1,000	52,436	78,543	158,276	672,626
24	23	1,000	57,177	87,497	183,168	842,033
25	24	1,000	62,249	97,347	211,793	1,053,791
26	25	1,000	67,676	108,182	244,712	1,318,489
27	26	1,000	73,484	120,100	282,569	1,649,361
28	27	1,000	79,698	133,210	326,104	2,062,952
29	28	1,000	86,347	147,631	376,170	2,579,939
30	29	1,000	93,461	163,494	433,745	3,226,174
31	30	1,000	101,073	180,943	499,957	4,033,968

It does look like a computer glitch but it isn't. Einstein is reputed to have said compound interest was the greatest discovery of the twentieth century and even if he didn't, it is.

Conclusion

Sensible investing is not difficult, it is just work. The less you get paid by the stock market in thrills and spills, the more you will earn at it in cash.

Value investing has been a very reliable method of making money in the stock market and it is a good place to start for people who want to build up wealth and don't want to be gamblers.

Value investing works because investors build up their skill in stock selection picking under-priced shares. They do not risk much of their money on any stock in particular and they know what they are buying and why. This puts the value investor in a small, smart and diligent group of people buying and selling shares and this select nature is a large part of why it is a successful way to make money from the stock market.

Meanwhile others punt shares on rumours for the hell of it and some never wonder why or even realise they are losing a lot of money. Gamblers are like that. However, gambling is not compulsory in the stock market and in fact gives plenty of opportunity for the careful and diligent to make money.

This book is about getting started, not all that can be known about value investing, and it is most certainly not the only way to make money from the market. It is, however, a sound platform to begin investing and one that you will never have to vacate. In the end if all the value investments were to disappear then for me it would be time to wonder if it was a good moment to sell up. This has only happened once to me, in 2006, and it didn't take long for the following market crash to deliver me the best selection of value investments I've ever seen.

The End

ABOUT THE AUTHOR

Clem Chambers is CEO of ADVFN, Europe and South America's leading financial website.

A broadcast and print media regular, Clem Chambers is a familiar face and frequent co-presenter on CNBC and CNBC Europe. He is a seasoned guest and market commentator on BBC News, Fox News, CNBC Arabia Newsnight, Al Jazeera, CNN, SKY News, TF1, Canada's Business News Network and numerous US radio stations.

He is renowned for calling the markets and predicted the end of the bull market back in January 2007 and the following crash. He has appeared on ITV's News at Ten and Evening News discussing failures in the banking system and featured prominently in the Money Programme's Credit Crash Britain: HBOS — Breaking the Bank and on the BBC's City Uncovered: When Markets Go Mad.

Clem has written investment columns for Wired Magazine, which described him as a 'Market Maven', The Daily Mail, The Daily Telegraph and The Daily Express and currently writes for The Scotsman, Forbes, RiskAFRICA, Traders and YTE.

He was The Alchemist – stock tipster – in The Business for over three years and has been published in titles including: CityAM, Investors Chronicle, Traders Magazine, Stocks and Commodities, the Channel 4 website, SFO and Accountancy Age and has been quoted in many more publications including all of the main UK national newspapers. He also wrote a monthly spread betting column in gambling magazine Inside Edge for over a year.

Clem has written several books for ADVFN Books, including 101 Ways To Pick Stock Market Winners and A Beginner's Guide to Value Investing.

In the last few years he has become a financial thriller writer, authoring The Twain Maxim, The Armageddon Trade, Kusanagi and The First Horseman.

Clem also writes for the ADVFN newspaper and has a premium newsletter.

ALSO BY CLEM CHAMBERS

Letters to my Broker
P.S. What do you think of the Market

by A. Kustomer and Clem Chambers

Joe, a rich but hapless investor, makes every mistake possible. Just when you think he's learnt something, he finds a new way to lose money. This classic comedy of errors revived for a new generation teaches that the rules to trading haven't changed in 94 years. Aided by the acerbic commentary of Clem Chambers, the book tells you where Joe's going wrong, what you should do to keep your shirt and how to avoid his hilarious errors. Read it and trade like it's 1919!

The Death of Wealth:
The Economic Fall of the West

by Clem Chambers

Was 2012 the beginning of the end for western wealth? Best-selling author and Forbes columnist Clem Chambers puts the markets in review and explains the forthcoming crises. Anthologising his writings from the past year, *The Death of Wealth* is the essential guide to the emerging financial landscape.

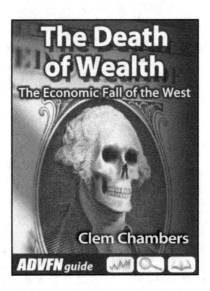

ADVFN Guide:
101 Ways to Pick Stock Market Winners

by Clem Chambers

101 tips to help day traders, investors and stock pickers to focus on what characterises a potentially successful stock. Personally researched by Clem Chambers, one of the world's leading authorities on market performance. Incisive, brutally honest and occasionally very funny, *101 Ways to Pick Stock Market Winners* is an invaluable manual for anyone wanting to make money out of the markets.

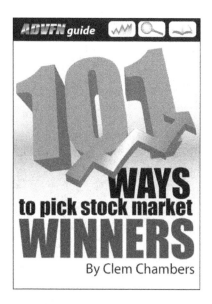

Go to www.advfnbooks.com for more information on these titles.

OTHER TITLES FROM ADVFN BOOKS

Lessons From The Financial Markets For 2013

by Zak Mir

Learn from all the suspense, mania and gloom of one of the markets' most dramatic years. In *Lessons From The Financial Markets For 2013* Zak Mir puts all his charting expertise to practice and analyses the key stocks, markets and events to provide an essential preview of 2013. By exploring the highlights and the lowlights of 2012 you can learn vital lessons to help make the best investment choices, now and in the future.

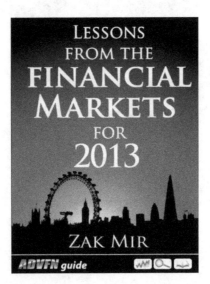

101 Charts for Trading Success

by Zak Mir

Using insider knowledge to reveal the tricks of the trade, Zak Mir's *101 Charts for Trading Success* explains the most complex set ups in the market. Illustrated with easy to understand charts this is the accessible, essential guide of how to read, understand and use charts to buy and sell stocks; a must for all future investment millionaires!

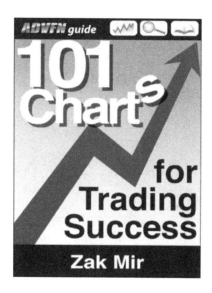

Lessons From The Trader Wizard

by Bill Cara

New from trading legend and the Free Market Patriot Bill Cara, *Lessons From The Trader Wizard* teaches the tactics and skills to beat Wall Street. Bill shows you how to navigate the new world of trading the capital markets.

Evil's Good:
Book of Boasts and Other Investments

by Simon Cawkwell

Britain's most feared bear-raider spots overvalued stocks, shorts them and goes for the kill. He's been known to make £500,000 in a single week. In *Evil's Good* – part auto-biography, part financial training guide – Simon Cawkwell tells all of his market triumphs (and downfalls) and describes the 'shorting' rules that have made him so wealthy.

Go to www.advfnbooks.com for more information on these titles.

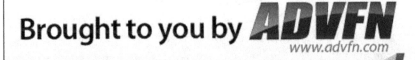

CPSIA information can be obtained
at www.ICGtesting.com
Printed in the USA
LVHW081617010620
657133LV00034B/2673

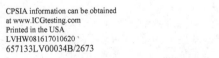

9 781908 756206